SCIENCE TIMELINES

THE RISE OF INDUSTRY

1700 - 1800

By Charlie Samuels

W
FRANKLIN WATTS
LONDON•SYDNEY

First published in Great Britain in 2015 by
The Watts Publishing Group

Copyright © 2015 Brown Bear Books Ltd

All rights reserved.

For Brown Bear Books Ltd:
Editorial Director: Lindsey Lowe
Managing Editor: Tim Cooke
Children's Publisher: Anne O'Daly
Design Manager: David Poole
Designer: Kim Browne
Picture Manager: Sophie Mortimer
Production Director: Alastair Gourlay

Dewey no. 509

ISBN: 978 1 4451 4258 6

Printed in China

Franklin Watts
An imprint of
Hachette Children's Group
Part of The Watts Publishing Group
Carmelite House
50 Victoria Embankment
London EC4Y 0DZ

An Hachette UK Company
www.hachette.co.uk

www.franklinwatts.co.uk

Contents

Introduction

The scientific developments of the 18th century shaped our modern world, introducing industrialisation, mass production and rapid transport.

Increasingly, the people who made scientific advances were professionals such as engineers. They saw scientific research as a tool for the advancement of business as well as for the improvement of the world. As always, advances often came through gradual steps. Iron had already been used for many centuries. Early in the 18th century, however, a new way to produce it made it much cheaper. That change was instrumental to developments such as the invention of steam engines, which pumped water from mines, and the building of railways. Water transport also improved, both at sea and with the construction of canal systems to move around the raw materials and manufactured goods of industry. In the countryside, agricultural machines helped farmers produce more food to support the growing populations of towns and cities.

Scientific and Social Changes

The profound changes in transport, manufacturing and production created great social change. For the first time, workers were brought together in large factories. Their work was increasingly done on machines, and the things they made were the first examples of mass production. At the end of the 18th century, both the United States and France underwent great political upheaval.

About This Book

This book uses timelines to describe scientific and technological advances from about 1700 to about 1800. A continuous timeline of the period runs along the bottom of all the pages. Its entries are colour-coded to indicate the different fields of science to which they belong. Each chapter also has its own subject timeline, which runs vertically down the edge of the page.

Underlying much of the Industrial Revolution was the development of cheaper ways of making iron in blast furnaces. The basic technology is still in use today.

Iron Smelting

Although ironworking had been known since early times, iron tools and weapons remained rare until the invention of the blast furnace in about 700 CE.

↑ A forge needs to produce great heat (over 900°C/1,600°F) to melt iron from its ore.

TIMELINE
1700–1705

KEY:

- Astronomy and Maths
- Biology and Medicine
- Chemistry and Physics
- Engineering and Invention

1700

1701

1702

1701 Italian physician Giacomo Pylarini inoculates three children in Constantinople with smallpox to prevent more serious disease when they are older.

1701 English agriculturalist Jethro Tull invents a mechanical seed drill for sowing seeds.

1702 English anatomist William Cowper discovers Cowper's glands in the male reproductive system.

1700 German mathematician Gottfried Leibniz founds the Berlin Academy, the first national academy of science.

1701 English astronomer Edmond Halley produces a map of the world showing magnetic variations.

The art of ironworking spread from ancient Egypt and Anatolia (modern Turkey) to India and China. Ancient Greeks used iron bolts to join blocks of stone, and in about 400 BCE, Chinese craftsmen made statues from a type of cast iron. The first blast furnace for iron, the Catalan forge in Spain, is thought to date from about 700 CE.

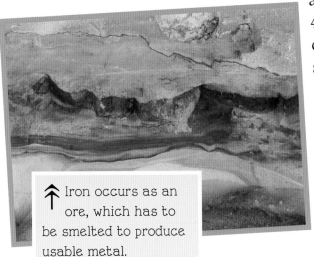

↑ Iron occurs as an ore, which has to be smelted to produce usable metal.

English Developments

By the 14th century, England was Europe's main iron-producing country. Waterwheels powered the bellows to produce a continuous stream of air for the blast furnaces, which could produce up to 3 metric tonnes (3.3 tons) of iron a day. This output required large amounts of charcoal, produced by burning wood. As a result, most of Britain's forests were destroyed. Then, in 1709, English iron

Timeline

700 The Catalan forge in Spain is the first blast furnace

1709 Coke in blast furnaces

1779 Iron bridge at Coalbrookdale

1828 Neilson's hot-air process

1857 Hot-blast stove

↓ This illustration shows workers in a 16th-century blast furnace; one man operates the bellows while the other melts the iron.

1703 English physicist Francis Hawksbee invents an improved vacuum pump.

1704 English scientist Isaac Newton publishes his book *Opticks*, about the nature and behaviour of light.

1703

1704

1705

1703 The Eddystone Lighthouse in the English Channel is washed away in a storm, killing its architect.

1704 Italian clockmaker Nicolas Fatio de Duiller makes a clock with jewel bearings.

How a Blast Furnace Works

Metalworkers made a furnace by digging a hole and adding a conical chimney. The furnace was filled with iron ore, limestone and charcoal, and set on fire. Bellows blasted air through the furnace. The ore was changed into metallic iron by the action of carbon monoxide (CO), itself formed by the action of air on the charcoal (carbon). The limestone helped trap impurities.

→ Metalworkers used bellows to force air into the furnace, raising the temperature and producing molten iron.

founder Abraham Darby began using coke (derived from coal) instead of charcoal. Darby's development had a dramatic effect on the production and uses of cast iron, and cast-iron pans, pots and kettles soon became common in every home in England.

Darby's Improvements

Darby built his furnaces at Coalbrookdale on the banks of the River Severn in western England. In 1742, his son, Abraham Darby II, installed a steam engine to pump water from the river to power the bellows. In 1779, Darby's grandson, Abraham Darby III, used prefabricated cast-iron sections to build a bridge over the Severn River at Coalbrookdale. It is 30 metres (98 feet) long and stands 12 metres (39 feet) above the water.

The final improvements to

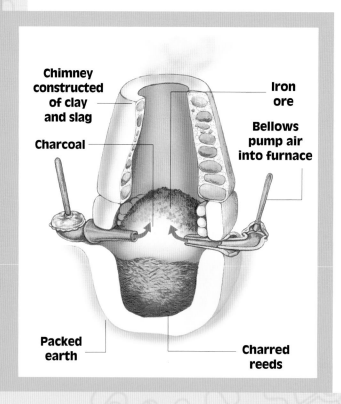

Chimney constructed of clay and slag

Charcoal

Iron ore

Bellows pump air into furnace

Packed earth

Charred reeds

TIMELINE
1705–1710

1706 English physicist Francis Hawksbee constructs an electrostatic generator.

1707 English physician John Floyer produces a special watch for counting patients' pulse rates.

KEY:

Astronomy and Maths

Biology and Medicine

Chemistry and Physics

Engineering and Invention

1705   1706   1707

1706 Welsh mathematician William Jones introduces the symbol pi for the ratio of the circumference of a circle to its diameter.

← The bridge over the Severn River at Coalbrookdale was built by Abraham Darby III in 1779. Travellers paid a toll to cross.

↓ The Coalbrookdale bridge was made from prefabricated cast-iron sections, bolted together on site.

the blast furnace came in the 1800s. In Glasgow, Scotland, in 1828, Scottish engineer James Neilson improved its efficiency by preheating the air by sending it through a red-hot tube. The tube was heated at first by a coal fire and later by coal gas, a by-product from furnaces. English inventor Edward Cowper improved Neilson's design in 1857 with his hot-blast stove, which used gases from the blast furnace itself to preheat the air.

1709 English physicist Francis Hawksbee describes capillary action, which causes sponges or blotting paper to soak up liquid.

1709 Polish-born Dutch physicist Gabriel Fahrenheit invents the alcohol thermometer and the Fahrenheit temperature scale.

1708   1709   1710

1708 German alchemist Johann Böttger invents hard-paste porcelain (previously, porcelain-making was known only to the Chinese).

1709 English iron founder Abraham Darby introduces the use of coke for iron smelting.

Navigation at Sea

The crew of a ship at sea needs to know what direction it is heading and its exact position. A compass shows direction, but exact position is more difficult to determine.

⟶ The sextant measured a ship's position north or south of the equator.

TIMELINE
1710-1715

1710 French chemist René-Antoine Ferchault de Réaumur creates a material woven entirely from glass fibre.

1712 English engineer Thomas Newcomen invents an atmospheric steam engine that employs a piston.

KEY:

- Astronomy and Maths
- Biology and Medicine
- Chemistry and Physics
- Engineering and Invention

1710   1711   1712

1711 Italian naturalist Luigi Marsigli shows that corals are animals (they were previously thought to be plants).

1712 Italian mathematician Giovanni Ceva applies mathematical principles to economics.

Latitude indicates a position in terms of its distance north or south of the equator. It is measured in degrees. For example, London is at a latitude of approximately 51.5° north. Latitude can be found by measuring the angle of a particular heavenly body above the horizon and consulting books of tables or almanacs. The angle of the Pole Star at night or the angle of the sun at noon can be measured and compared with tables. Early sailors had various instruments for measuring these angles. Using a cross-staff, a sailor sighted along a 1-metre- (3-foot-) long staff while moving a crosspiece until the lower end lined up with the horizon and the upper end coincided with the star or the sun. The staff was calibrated in degrees from which the sailor could read off the angle. It was first described by the astronomer Levi ben Gershom (1288–1344) and was used in Europe until the 18th century.

Navigators' Tools

In 1594, English sailor John Davis (c.1550–1605) invented the backstaff. It was pointed in the opposite direction, so the operator did not need to look directly into the sun.

Timeline
1594 Backstaff

1731 Octant

1735 Chronometer

1757 Sextant

1759 Harrison's prize-winning chronometer

↓ Sailors used charts from the 13th century as guides to sea coasts.

1714 The first typewriter is invented by English engineer Henry Mill, but no one now knows how it worked.

1715 The English clockmaker John Harrison invents a clock that runs for eight days on a single winding.

1713   1714   1715

1714 French physician Dominique Anel invents a fine-point syringe for medical procedures.

1714 The British government offers a prize of £20,000 to the first person to devise a method of measuring longitude at sea – the prize is not claimed until 1759.

How the Sextant Works

A navigator uses a sextant to measure the angle of the sun (or a prominent star) above the horizon. Tables convert the angle into the navigator's latitude. The index glass (in fact, a mirror) reflects the sun's rays onto the horizon glass. This half-mirror reflects the rays along a telescope to the navigator's eye. The navigator also looks through the plain (unsilvered) half of the horizon glass at the horizon and adjusts the angle of the index glass until the sun's image appears to be on the horizon. The graduated scale on the limb of the sextant then indicates the angle of the sun above the horizon.

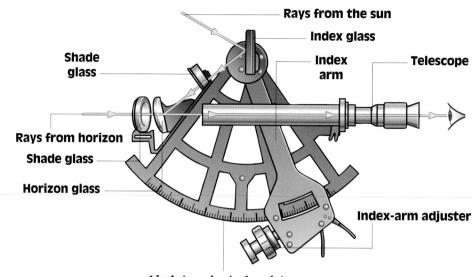

Rays from the sun

Index glass

Shade glass

Index arm

Telescope

Rays from horizon

Shade glass

Horizon glass

Index-arm adjuster

Limb (graduated scale)

↑ This diagram shows the key parts of a sextant; the box (left) tells you how it worked.

The quadrant was a similar instrument, also used by astronomers and by gunners to set the correct angles for aiming artillery pieces.

Then, in 1731, English mathematician John Hadley (1682–1744) invented the octant, incorrectly named Hadley's quadrant at the time. Anglo-American inventor Thomas Godfrey (1704–1749) of Philadelphia invented an almost identical instrument independently. In the octant, a pivoted arm carries a mirror that can be moved to bring an image of the sun in line with another mirror. The second mirror also gives a view of the horizon. The maximum angle it could measure was 45°.

TIMELINE
1715–1720

KEY:

Astronomy and Maths

Biology and Medicine

Chemistry and Physics

Engineering and Invention

1716 English astronomer Edmund Halley invents the diving bell, so that workers can build construction foundations under water.

1716 French engineer Hubert Gautier publishes a book that is very influential on bridge design.

1717 Italian physician Giovanni Lancisi blames malaria on mosquito bites.

1715

1716

1717

1716 The first lighthouse is built in North America, in Boston Harbor.

1717 English astronomer Abraham Sharp calculates the value of pi to 72 decimal places.

From there it was a simple step to the sextant (which measured up to 60°), introduced by Scottish naval officer John Campbell (c.1720–1790) in 1757. This remained the standard navigational instrument for 250 years. It was even used on aircraft until it was finally supplanted by radio beacons and the satellite-based GPS (global positioning system).

↑ Sextants are still used to check the accuracy of modern navigation systems.

↓ Although the design of the sextant has become more modern, the basic technology remains exactly the same as when it was introduced in 1757. It locates its user on Earth by measuring the position of objects in the heavens.

Finding Longitude

In 1884, an international conference agreed that the prime meridian (longitude 0°) should be the Greenwich meridian, which runs through Greenwich Observatory in London. The longitude of any other place is its position east or west of the Greenwich meridian. This proved to be far more difficult to work out

1718 English astronomer Edmund Halley identifies stellar proper motion, the gradual movement of stars relative to the sun.

1719 English mathematician Brook Taylor demonstrates the principle of the vanishing point in linear perspective.

1718

1719

1720

1718 French mathematician Abraham de Moivre writes a book on probability, *The Doctrine of Chances*.

1718 English inventor James Puckle patents a flintlock semiautomatic cannon.

1719 German engraver Jakob Le Blon invents a four-colour printing process using blue, yellow, red and black.

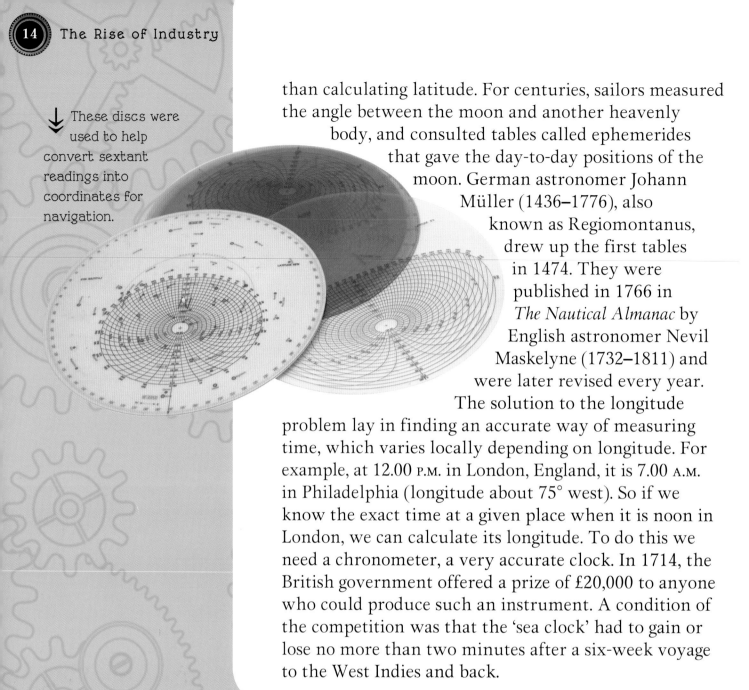

These discs were used to help convert sextant readings into coordinates for navigation.

than calculating latitude. For centuries, sailors measured the angle between the moon and another heavenly body, and consulted tables called ephemerides that gave the day-to-day positions of the moon. German astronomer Johann Müller (1436–1776), also known as Regiomontanus, drew up the first tables in 1474. They were published in 1766 in *The Nautical Almanac* by English astronomer Nevil Maskelyne (1732–1811) and were later revised every year.

The solution to the longitude problem lay in finding an accurate way of measuring time, which varies locally depending on longitude. For example, at 12.00 P.M. in London, England, it is 7.00 A.M. in Philadelphia (longitude about 75° west). So if we know the exact time at a given place when it is noon in London, we can calculate its longitude. To do this we need a chronometer, a very accurate clock. In 1714, the British government offered a prize of £20,000 to anyone who could produce such an instrument. A condition of the competition was that the 'sea clock' had to gain or lose no more than two minutes after a six-week voyage to the West Indies and back.

TIMELINE
1720–1725

1720 Italian harpsichord maker Bartolomeo Cristofori invents the pianoforte (piano).

1721 American physician Zabdiel Boylston carries out the first smallpox inoculation in the United States.

KEY:

Astronomy and Maths

Biology and Medicine

Chemistry and Physics

Engineering and Invention

1720   1721   1722

1720 English inventor Christopher Pinchbeck produces an alloy of copper and zinc; named pinchbeck, it resembles gold and is used in watches and jewellery.

English clockmaker John Harrison (1693–1776) took up the challenge, and in 1735 introduced his first chronometer. But it was his fourth instrument, which he made in 1759, that won the prize (or half of it, since the government kept half the money until Harrison showed that the chronometer could be copied). He did not receive the remainder of the money until 1773, and then only after King George III pleaded Harrison's case.

⬆ This stone marks the prime meridian, 0° longitude, at Greenwich in London.

Finding Longitude

Finding a ship's east–west position needs an accurate chronometer. If a ship sails from Greenwich at noon, its chronometer is set to 12 o'clock. After five days, at noon local time (gauged by sextant) the chronometer reads 4.00 P.M. The Earth has rotated on its axis for four hours since it was 12 o'clock in Greenwich. The four hours represent 4/24, or 1/6, of a complete rotation, or 1/6 of 360°, or 60°.

⬅ In this example, the ship's position is 60° west

START OF JOURNEY

N

Chronometer 12 o'clock

Local time 12 o'clock

90°W
60°W
30°W
0°

S

AFTER 5 DAYS' SAILING

N

Chronometer 4 o'clock

Local time 12 o'clock

90°W
60°W
30°W
0°

S

1724 Peter the Great founds the St Petersburg Academy of Sciences in Russia.

1725 German physicist Johann Schulze notices that some silver salts turn dark in daylight: the discovery will be significant in the development of photography.

1723

1724

1725

1723 French engineer Nicolas Bion writes a catalogue of surveying instruments currently in use.

1724 Dutch scientist Hermann Boerhaave publishes *Element of Chemistry,* the first major chemistry textbook.

1725 French clockmaker Antoine Thiout constructs a clock that displays solar time.

Benjamin Franklin

Benjamin Franklin played an important part in the development of the United States, but he also made major discoveries in physics and was a talented inventor.

➔ Franklin is said to have tested the electrical nature of lightning by flying a kite in a storm.

TIMELINE
1725–1730

KEY:

- Astronomy and Maths
- Biology and Medicine
- Chemistry and Physics
- Engineering and Invention

1725 Scottish goldsmith William Ged invents stereotype printing, in which a mould is made of a complete page.

1727 Swiss mathematician Leonhard Euler introduces the symbol *e* as the base of natural logarithms.

1725   1726   1727

1726 English clockmaker George Graham invents the mercury pendulum for clocks, which does not change length with a change in temperature.

1727 English botanist Stephen Hales writes *Vegetable Staticks*, the first book on plant physiology.

Born in Boston into a family of 17 children, Benjamin Franklin left school at the age of ten. Two years later, he was apprenticed to his older brother James, a printer. When he was just 18, Benjamin took over publication of the *New England Courant*, a weekly newspaper founded by James. He did not stay for long; instead, he went to Philadelphia and worked as a printer himself. In 1724, he set sail for England. He returned home two years later and published the first volume of *Poor Richard's Almanac* in 1733, a collection of articles on a wide range of subjects to 'convey instruction among the common people'. He held various public offices and helped draft the Declaration of Independence in 1776. He travelled to France to raise help for the American revolutionaries, or 'rebels', and while in Paris he witnessed the Montgolfier brothers' first hot-air balloon flight in 1783. He was a staunch supporter of the abolition of slavery; he retired from public life in 1788.

➤➤ As a politician, Franklin was one of the leading Founders of the United States.

Franklin and Electricity

During his lifetime, Franklin also conducted scientific experiments. The best known, in 1752, was one of the most dangerous experiments ever undertaken.

Timeline

1733 *Poor Richard's Almanac* first published

1742 Franklin stove

1752 Kite experiment and lightning rod

1784 Bifocal eyeglasses

1728 English clockmaker John Harrison invents the gridiron pendulum for clocks; its length is not affected by changes in temperature.

1729 English physicist Stephen Gray distinguishes between electrical insulators and conductors.

1728   1729   1730

1728 US naturalist John Bartram opens the first botanical gardens in America, near Philadelphia.

1728 French dentist Pierre Fauchard invents the first dental drill and makes the first fillings.

1730 French surgeon George Martin performs the first tracheostomy, an operation to make a hole in the windpipe.

Hearth and Home

At a domestic level, Franklin is credited with inventing the rocking chair and, in 1742, the Franklin stove, which had an underfloor draughtpipe. Franklin needed spectacles for reading and different glasses for distance vision. Annoyed with always having to change glasses, he invented bifocals in about 1784. They had split lenses – the upper half for distance vision and the lower half for near vision. In a bid to save fuel on dark evenings, he suggested the introduction of daylight saving time.

He attached a metal key to the moistened string of a kite, which he flew during a thunderstorm. Electric 'fluid' flowing down the string caused sparks to jump between the key and a Leyden jar (a primitive electrical condenser). Franklin had established the electrical nature of lightning and he coined the words 'positive' and 'negative' to describe the two types of static electricity. Several European scientists who tried to repeat the experiment were struck by lightning and killed. Franklin, however, devised a means of protection: he invented the lightning rod, a pointed conductor located at the top of a building and connected to the ground by a thick wire attached to a plate buried in the soil. Today, all tall buildings have lightning rods. Franklin theorised that thunderclouds are electrically charged and recognised

↑ Franklin invented bifocals, which improve both distance and near vision.

TIMELINE
1730-1735

KEY:
- Astronomy and Maths
- Biology and Medicine
- Chemistry and Physics
- Engineering and Invention

1730 English mathematician John Hadley devises the quadrant, an instrument for navigation.

1731 English agriculturalist Jethro Tull recommends modern farming methods in an influential book.

1730

1731

1732

1730 French chemist René-Antoine Ferchault de Réaumur makes an alcohol thermometer.

1731 English astronomer John Bevis discovers the Crab Nebula.

1732 French physicist Henri Pitot creates the Pitot tube, an instrument for measuring speed of airflow.

the aurora borealis (the northern lights, visible in the sky at polar latitudes) to be electrical in nature.

Other Scientific Interests

Franklin had many other scientific interests. Unlike most of his contemporaries, he rejected Newton's corpuscular theory of light (that light travels as particles), favouring the wave theories of Robert Hooke and others. He suggested that the rapid heating of air near warm ground causes it to expand and spiral upwards, producing tornadoes and waterspouts. He investigated the course of the Gulf Stream, the current of warm water that flows across the Atlantic Ocean, and he suggested that ships' captains should use a thermometer to locate and benefit from the current (or avoid it, depending on the direction in which they were sailing). In 1824, the Franklin Institute was founded in Philadelphia in his honour.

↓ This cutaway diagram shows the flue that provided the backdraught to make the Franklin stove so efficient.

1733 English engineer John Kay invents the flying shuttle, which speeds up the process of weaving.

1734 French chemist René-Antoine Ferchault de Réaumur writes *Memoirs Serving as a Natural History of Insects*, which founds the science of entomology.

1735 Swedish naturalist Carolus Linnaeus classifies objects into three classes: animal, plant or mineral.

1733   1734   1735

1733 French mathematician Abraham de Moivre discovers the normal (bell-shaped) distribution curve, which is now a major element in statistical studies.

1734 Swedish scientist Emanuel Swedenborg writes *Mineral Kingdom*, describing techniques for mining and smelting metals.

The Steam Engine

Humans relied on wind, water or animal power for energy until the invention of the steam engine, which culminated in 1765 with the work of James Watt.

→ Mines used steam engines to run pumps that removed water from under ground.

TIMELINE
1735-1740

KEY:

- Astronomy and Maths
- Biology and Medicine
- Chemistry and Physics
- Engineering and Invention

1735 Spanish scientist Antonio de Ulloa rediscovers platinum in South America.

1735 English physicist Stephen Gray suggests that lightning is an electrical phenomenon.

1737 Swedish chemist Georg Brandt discovers cobalt, the first completely new metal discovered since ancient times.

1735   1736   1737

1735 English clockmaker John Harrison makes a chronometer, a clock that keeps time well enough to be used to calculate longitude at sea.

1736 French surveyor Alexis Clairaut measures the length of 1 degree of meridian (longitude), allowing accurate calculation of the size of Earth.

The earliest steam engines are more accurately called atmospheric engines: they used the pressure of the air. The first was devised by French physicist Denis Papin. A vertical, open-ended cylinder with a close-fitting piston had water inside its base. A fire heated the base of the cylinder, causing the water to boil and turn into steam. Steam pressure lifted the piston, which remained raised while the cylinder cooled. The steam condensed back to liquid water, creating a partial vacuum in the cylinder. Then atmospheric pressure on the upper end of the piston pushed it down again. A rope connected to the piston and moving over a pulley could be used to lift a load or work a pump.

Savery's Steam Pump

A similar arrangement, patented in 1698 by English mining engineer Thomas Savery, turned the atmospheric engine into a practical steam pump. It had no piston or other moving parts, just hand-operated valves to provide continuous operation. Steam from a boiler passed into a working chamber that was sprayed with cold water to condense the steam. The partial vacuum that was created as a result lifted water through a one-way valve into the chamber. Steam was then let in again, which forced the water out and up through another one-way valve.

Timeline

1690 Papin's primitive engine

1698 Savery's atmospheric steam pump

1712 Newcomen's atmospheric steam engine

1765 Watt's engine with external condenser

1801 Trevithick's high-pressure engine

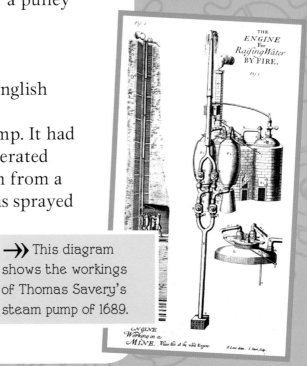

➤➤ This diagram shows the workings of Thomas Savery's steam pump of 1689.

1738 English inventor Lewis Paul produces a machine for carding wool, or combing it into parallel fibres.

1738 English metallurgist William Champion devises a new industrial process for the extraction of zinc from its ores.

1740 English metallurgist Benjamin Huntsman invents the crucible process for making steel in batches.

1738   1739   1740

1738 Swiss scientist Daniel Bernoulli suggests that the behaviour of gases is explained if they are made up of tiny particles of matter.

Newcomen's Steam Engine

In Newcomen's engine, steam from a boiler forced a piston up an open-ended cylinder; cold water sprayed into the cylinder condensed the steam, creating a partial vacuum that sucked the piston down again. The piston joined to one end of a long beam; the other end of the beam connected to a pump. As the piston went up and down, the beam rocked and worked the pump continuously.

➤ Newcomen's engine used steam to push the piston directly, unlike atmospheric engines.

In 1712, English engineer Thomas Newcomen perfected the first engine to use steam pressure to work a piston. They were usually called beam engines. Newcomen could not patent his engine because its principle was too close to that of Thomas Savery's, so the two men went into partnership.

This was the stage that steam power had reached in 1764, when Scottish engineer James Watt received a model of a Newcomen engine to repair. He realised how much energy was wasted by first heating the cylinder and then cooling it. In 1765, he added a separate external condenser. In addition, he used steam to push up the piston and then – by admitting low-pressure steam on the other side – to push it down again. This double action greatly

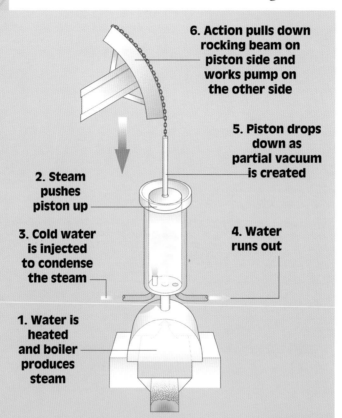

6. Action pulls down rocking beam on piston side and works pump on the other side

5. Piston drops down as partial vacuum is created

2. Steam pushes piston up

4. Water runs out

3. Cold water is injected to condense the steam

1. Water is heated and boiler produces steam

TIMELINE
1740–1745

1740 Swiss naturalist Charles Bonnet observes parthenogenesis in aphids, in which unfertilised females give birth.

1742 American scientist and politician Benjamin Franklin invents a wood-burning stove.

KEY:

- Astronomy and Maths
- Biology and Medicine
- Chemistry and Physics
- Engineering and Invention

1740　　　　　1741　　　　　1742

1741 Swedish engineer Christoph Polhem introduces a gear-cutting machine.

1742 Swedish astronomer Anders Celsius introduces the 100-degree Celsius (or centigrade) temperature scale.

improved the efficiency of the machine.

Trevithick's Engines

The next development became available by 1800, when Watt's master patent expired. The following year, English inventor Richard Trevithick started building double-action, high-pressure engines. Trevithick removed the separate condenser and used the waste steam to preheat the water entering the boiler. Within four years, he built nearly 50 engines that were used mainly in mines in Britain and eventually in countries in South America.

By their very action, early steam engines produced an up-and-down motion. But most machines of the time, except pumps, required rotary motion. Until the advent of the steam engine, most of them had been driven by waterwheels. Then, in 1781, James Watt invented the sun-and-planet gear to make his engines provide a rotary final drive.

⬆ Newcomen's engine and its rocking arm were so large they filled a whole building.

⬇ Richard Trevithick developed the highly efficient double-action, high-pressure engine.

1743 The American Philosophical Society is founded.

1743 English metalworker Thomas Boulsover produces 'Sheffield plate', metalware consisting of copper coated with a thin layer of silver.

1745 French surgeon Jacques Daviel successfully performs an operation for the removal of a cataract from a patient's eye.

1743

1744

1745

1743 English mathematician Thomas Simpson devises a systematic approach to finding the area bounded by a curve.

1745 Russian scientist Mikhail Lomonosov compiles a catalog of more than 300 minerals.

James Watt

One of history's greatest engineers, James Watt produced the first reliable engines to power textile mills and pump water out of mines.

⟫ The key to Watt's engine was the condenser (the small cylinder at left).

TIMELINE
1745–1750

1745 Dutch physicist Pieter van Musschenbroek invents the Leyden jar, a simple form of electrical condenser.

1747 French monk Jean-Antoine Nollet devises an electrometer (an instrument for measuring electrical charge).

1747 Scottish physician James Lind experiments with citrus fruits to prevent scurvy among sailors in the British Royal Navy.

1746 English chemist John Roebuck develops the lead-chamber process for making sulphuric acid.

1745   1746   1747

KEY:

Astronomy and Maths

Biology and Medicine

Chemistry and Physics

Engineering and Invention

← In legend, Watt was inspired to make a steam engine by watching a kettle boil.

Timeline

1765 Steam engine with separate condenser

1769 Watt patents his steam engine

1775 Partnership with Matthew Boulton

1781 Sun-and-planet gear

1782 Double-acting steam engine

1788 Flying-ball governor

Scottish engineer James Watt (1736–1819) learned technical skills from his father, a carpenter. In 1755, Watt worked in London as apprentice to a maker of mathematical instruments. Two years later, he was appointed instrument maker at Glasgow University and had his own workshop.

Improving the Steam Engine

The university had a model of a Newcomen steam engine, and in 1764 Watt was asked to repair it. He realised that the alternate heating and cooling processes of the cylinder wasted a lot of energy: it was heated by steam and then cooled by cold water sprayed into the cylinder to condense the steam.

In 1765, Watt made an engine that overcame the difficulty by leading the steam into a separate condenser so that the cylinder could remain hot all the time,

↑ James Watt performs an experiment in his workshop.

1748 Scottish physician John Fothergill gives the first description of diphtheria.

1750 French astronomer Guillaume Le Gentil de la Galasière discovers the Trifid Nebula in the constellation Sagittarius.

1748

1749

1750

1748 English astronomer James Bradley discovers the nutation of Earth, or the slight nodding of Earth's axis as it orbits.

1749 Carolus Linnaeus introduces binomial (two-part) naming for animals and plants, using genus and species names.

making the engine three times more efficient. Watt moved to England, and in 1775 went into business with Matthew Boulton to manufacture Watt's engine, which he had patented in 1769.

The first machine of 1776 needed five years of development before it was reliable enough for quantity production, and Watt constantly fought legal battles over infringement of his patent. Most of the engines he made were used as pumps to replace the 50-year-old Newcomen engines in tin and copper mines.

Constant Improvements

Watt worked to improve his engine. In order to convert the up-and-down motion of the piston into rotary motion, he invented the sun-and-planet gear and the connecting rod-and-crank system in 1781. Such innovations by Watt made the engine more useful for driving lathes, looms and cranes.

In 1782, Watt produced a double-acting steam engine in which steam is let in alternately on each side of the piston. The machine used steam power on every stroke. He devised the flying-ball centrifugal governor in 1788 to control an engine's speed. His invention of the pressure gauge in 1790 completed his engine, and by the end of the 18th century there were

↑ James Watt is remembered in the international unit of power, the watt, which was named after him.

TIMELINE
1750–1755

1751 On an expedition to the Cape of Good Hope, French astronomer Nicolas de Lacaille makes observations that enable the first accurate calculations of the distance from Earth to the moon.

1752 American scientist and politician Benjamin Franklin demonstrates the electrical nature of lightning in a famous kite-flying experiment.

KEY:
1750   1751   1752

Astronomy and Maths

Biology and Medicine

Chemistry and Physics

Engineering and Invention

1750 German engineer Johann Segner constructs a waterwheel in which the wheel is turned by the force of a jet of water.

1751 Swedish chemist Axel Cronstedt discovers nickel.

1752 French chemist René-Antoine Ferchault de Réaumur discovers how gastric juices operate in digestion.

nearly 500 Watt engines in use. Their output was measured in units called horsepower, another of Watt's innovations.

Watt's other achievements included a method of copying documents using a special ink. This hectograph was patented in 1780.

Another of his inventions was a sculpting machine for reproducing busts and figures. In 1794, he became a founder of the new company of Boulton, Watt and Sons. Watt retired in 1800 and lived to see his son, James Watt Jr, receive acclaim in 1817 for making the engines for the *Caledonia*, the first sea-going steamship to leave an English port.

← Watt invented a machine for copying ancient busts like this portrait of Aristotle.

The Centrifugal Governor

James Watt devised the governor to control his steam engines. (see picture below left). A belt (1), driven by the engine, rotates a vertical shaft on the governor. As it turns, it flings the weights (2) outwards by centrifugal force. As they go round, they rise (3), lifting the rod (4). The rod works a valve that controls the supply of steam to the engine. Reducing the supply slows the engine; but as it slows, the rod gradually falls and lets in more steam. This is an example of feedback control.

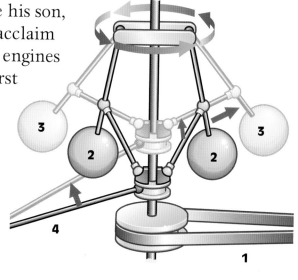

→ Watt's centrifugal governor made sure that an engine did not operate too fast.

1755 German philosopher Immanuel Kant proposes a theory that the solar system was created from a spinning gaseous nebula and that our galaxy is just one of many in the universe.

1753   1754   1755

1753 Scottish engineer Charles Morrison invents a 26-wire telegraph (one wire for each letter of the Roman alphabet).

Textiles

Textile machinery was at the forefront of the Industrial Revolution. Within just 70 years, the Western textile industry became totally mechanised.

↑ The loom lifts warp threads to allow weft threads to be passed between them.

TIMELINE
1755–1760

1756 English engineer John Smeaton invents 'hydraulic lime', cement that hardens under water.

1757 English engineer Henry Berry builds the Sankey Brook Navigation, the first modern canal.

1757 English clockmaker Thomas Mudge invents a lever escapement for a watch, which is first used in 1770.

KEY:

Astronomy and Maths

Biology and Medicine

Chemistry and Physics

Engineering and Invention

1755   1756   1757

The development of the mechanical spinning mule – the key to mechanisation of the textile industry – from the hand-operated spinning wheel took more than 600 years. After that, mechanisation was rapid.

The first aid to spinning was the distaff, which consists of a long stick onto which wool is loosely wound. The spinner (or spinster), in most cultures usually a woman, held the distaff under her arm and teased out a continuous strand of wool, which she spun between the fingers of the other hand. The spun thread wound itself around a rotating spindle at the end of the distaff. Historians have learned that the ancient Mesopotamians used the distaff 7,500 years ago, and it competes with the wheel as the oldest-known invention.

↑ Cotton fibres, like those of wool, need to be twisted into yarn in order to be used.

→ This spinning wheel has a foot treadle, so that the spinner can work sitting down.

Timeline

1200s Spinning wheel

1733 Flying shuttle

1764 Spinning jenny

1769 Spinning frame

1779 Spinning mule

1785 Steam-powered loom

1758 Halley's comet returns, as predicted by Edmond Halley in 1682.

1758 English weaver Jedediah Strutt invents the stocking frame, for making hosiery.

1758   1759   1760

1758 French astronomer Charles Messier rediscovers the Crab Nebula and designates it M1 in his catalogue of nebulas.

1758 German chemist Andreas Marggraf introduces flame tests to chemical analysis (various elements burn different colours).

The Loom

A loom consists of a frame to hold sets of parallel warp threads. The weft (crosswise) thread is wound on a shuttle, which the weaver works in and out of the lengthwise threads. Another frame, the heddle, holds vertical wires ending in rings through which the warp threads move. Controlled by treadles, the heddle lifts various sets of warp threads to create different kinds of weave.

→ This diagram shows the parts of a loom; the finished cloth is wound in a roll underneath.

Making Yarn

The spinning wheel, which was in regular use in Europe from the 1200s, simplified the task by using a large vertical wheel to wind the yarn. It had a belt drive to spin the spindle, while the spinner pulled a strand of wool from a vertical distaff. With her other hand she turned the wheel, although this task was mechanised by the addition of a foot treadle in the 16th century. The rocking motion of the treadle turned an upright wheel.

Two major advances came in the 18th century during the earliest stages of the Industrial Revolution. The English mechanic James Hargreaves (c.1720–1778) invented the

↑ The spinning jenny allowed a worker to spin many strands of yarn at the same time.

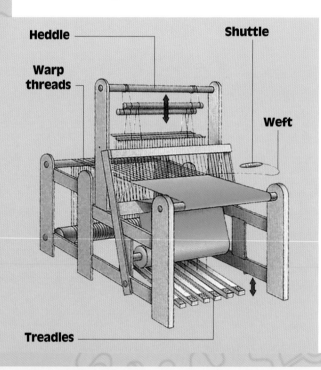

Heddle

Warp threads

Shuttle

Weft

Treadles

TIMELINE 1760-1765

1760 Swiss physicist Johann Lambert formulates Lambert's law, about the angle and brightness of reflected light.

1761 English engineer James Brindley completes the construction of the Bridgewater Canal near Manchester, England.

1762 The French open the world's first national veterinary college.

KEY:

1760   1761   1762

- Astronomy and Maths
- Biology and Medicine
- Chemistry and Physics
- Engineering and Invention

1761 Russian scientist Mikhail Lomonosov observes a transit of Venus across the sun and deduces that Venus has an atmosphere.

1761 Italian physician Giovanni Morgagni founds the science of pathology, or understanding disease.

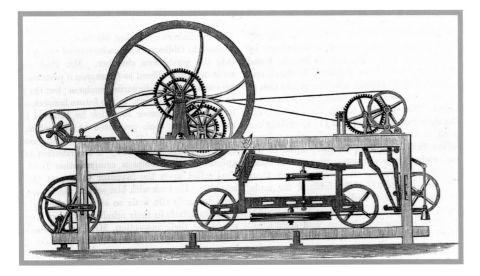

← Samuel Crompton's spinning mule allowed one spinner to produce 48 strands of fine yarn simultaneously.

spinning jenny in 1764 (he patented his device in 1770), and the spinning frame was invented by his compatriot Richard Arkwright (1732–1792) in 1769. The spinning jenny was originally turned by hand and was mostly used to produce woollen yarn (eight threads at once on the first machines). The spinning frame was powered by a waterwheel (early cotton and woollen mills usually stood on streams for that reason) and made cotton yarn strong enough to act as the warp (lengthwise) threads used in weaving.

The two ideas – the jenny and the spinning frame – were brought together in 1779 by English weaver Samuel Crompton (1753–1827), who invented what became known as the spinning mule. It produced 48 strands of yarn at the same time. It is said to have been named 'mule' because it was a hybrid of the two earlier machines (a mule is a cross between a horse and an ass).

1764 English mechanic James Hargreaves invents the spinning jenny for spinning many threads of cotton or wool at the same time. It is a key step in the Industrial Revolution.

1764 Italian-born French mathematician Joseph Lagrange explains why the motion of the moon allows us to see more than 50 per cent of its surface.

1763   1764   1765

1763 German botanist Josef Kölreuter discovers the role of insects in the pollination of flowers.

1764 French engineer Pierre Trésaguet introduces a new system of road building in France.

Rovings into Threads

In principle, these machines are much the same in their operation. The textile fibres, known as rovings, are wound onto rotating spindles that move on a frame. The frame first pulls the strands outwards, twisting them to form yarn; it then moves back while the yarn is wound onto bobbins. After 1828, cotton was usually spun on the ring-spinning frame invented by the American John Thorpe. The rovings go through a set of high-speed rollers that draw them into fine threads. Each thread then moves through a hole in a 'traveller', which twists the thread as it winds it onto a rapidly rotating vertical bobbin.

Mechanising Weaving

Having produced the yarn, the weaver then has to make it into cloth by weaving the threads together. This is the function of the loom. At its simplest, the loom is a frame that holds a set of parallel threads called the warp. The weaver interweaves them at right angles with another thread – known as the weft – that is carried on a bobbin in a boat-shaped holder known as a shuttle. The first improvement was the addition of cords that pulled up every other warp

↑ Just a handful of workers look after a mill full of cotton mules.

TIMELINE
1765–1770

KEY:

Astronomy and Maths

Biology and Medicine

Chemistry and Physics

Engineering and Invention

1765 The world's first mining academy is opened in Freiberg, Germany.

1766 French chemist Pierre Macquer publishes the first systematic dictionary of chemistry.

1765

1766

1767

1765 American scientist John Winthrop attempts to calculate the masses of comets.

1765 Scottish engineer James Watt builds a steam engine with a separate condenser.

1766 English scientist Henry Cavendish identifies hydrogen, which he calls 'inflammable air'.

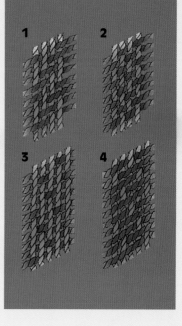

Different Patterns of Weaves

A loom produces different kinds of weave depending on the combination of warp threads lifted by the heddle, or frame. Shown here are sateen weave (1), satin weave (2), twill weave (3) and plain weave (4).

⬆ Children walk to work at a mill. Children were used to look after machines.

thread to make it easier to pass the shuttle from side to side. Soon weavers added treadles to work the cords.

The process of weaving sped up greatly in 1733 when the English engineer John Kay (1704–c.1780) invented the so-called flying shuttle, a mechanism that enables the weaver to 'throw' the shuttle rapidly from side to side of the loom through the warp threads. Mechanised looms came next, driven by waterpower at first, then by steam engines after 1785, the year that English inventor Edmund Cartwright (1743–1823) created the first steam-powered loom.

1769 English manufacturer Richard Arkwright produces the spinning frame for spinning strong cotton thread.

1769 English explorer James Cook leads an expedition to Tahiti to observe a transit of Venus across the sun's disc.

1768

1769

1770

1768 French chemist Antoine Baumé invents a hydrometer and a new density scale for graduating it.

1769 English chemist Joseph Priestly formulates his first laws about the nature of electrical forces.

1770 English chemist Joseph Priestly invents the pencil eraser.

Farm Machinery

Farming technology was generally ancient until cast-iron ploughshares appeared in the West towards the end of the 18th century.

→» This combine thresher was pulled by 30 horses and needed four men to operate it.

TIMELINE
1770-1775

1771 Italian physician Luigi Galvini shows that the muscles of a dissected frog twitch when they are stimulated by electricity.

1772 Scottish chemist Daniel Rutherford discovers nitrogen.

KEY:

Astronomy and Maths

Biology and Medicine

Chemistry and Physics

Engineering and Invention

1770   1771   1772

1770 French watchmaker Abraham-Louis Perrelet develops a watch with automatic winding.

1772 French mineralogist Jean Romé de l'Isle argues that crystals have constant angles between their faces.

1772 Swedish chemist Karl Scheele discovers oxygen but does not publish his findings until 1777.

Cast-iron ploughshares were invented in England and the United States in the 1780s and 1790s. Pulled by horses, they could cut through the soil deeper than could wooden ploughs. A plough made completely of cast iron was invented in 1819 and produced in quantity in 1839 by the American industrialist John Deere. By 1862, Dutch farmers were using steam traction engines to winch ploughshares in wheeled frames back and forth across a field. Other farmers used steam tractors to pull standard ploughs.

↑ This scene from the late 1700s shows a plough, a roller, a harrow and a seed drill.

Stages of the Harvest

Planting seed became mechanised by the invention of the seed drill in 1701. After harvesting, crops such as wheat had to be threshed to remove the grain; this was mechanised by the threshing machine in 1786. The last major farming process to be mechanised was reaping.

Timeline

1701 Mechanical seed drill

1785 Cast-iron ploughshare

1786 Threshing machine

1819 Cast-iron plough

1834 Reaping machine

1838 Combine harvester

1878 Binding machine

1908 Steam caterpillar tractor

1935 All-crop harvester

1773 German-born English astronomer William Herschel works out that the sun is gradually moving through space.

1774 English chemist Joseph Priestley identifies oxygen and publishes his findings.

1774 English engineer John Wilkinson patents a precision cannon-boring machine.

1773   1774   1775

1774 English astronomer Nevil Maskelyne calculates the average density of Earth.

1774 French chemist Antoine Lavoisier demonstrates the law of the conservation of mass in a chemical reaction.

Jethro Tull's Seed Drill

The mechanical seed drill was invented in 1701 by English agriculturist Jethro Tull (1674–1741). Using this machine, the farmer sowed the seed in parallel rows, making the crop easier to weed by hoeing and easier to harvest.

← Harvesting wheat was backbreaking work before the advent of farm machinery.

↑ This early 20th-century seed drill worked in the same way as Tull's original.

Credit usually goes to US engineer Cyrus McCormick, who patented a reaper in 1834 and soon produced them on a large scale. In 1879, he created the McCormick Harvesting Machine Company, which owned a factory in Chicago that made 4,000 machines a year. In 1827, Scottish clergyman Patrick Bell had invented a reaper and sent four examples to the United States. In 1833, US engineer Obed Hussey invented yet another type of reaper. His improved machine of 1847 was better than McCormick's for reaping grass and making hay,

TIMELINE
1775–1780

1775 German geologist Abraham Werner proposes – wrongly – the theory that the rocks in Earth's crust were created by the action of water.

1776 American inventor David Bushnell builds the *Turtle,* one of the first submarines.

KEY:

Astronomy and Maths

Biology and Medicine

Chemistry and Physics

Engineering and Invention

1775   1776   1777

1775 Danish naturalist Johann Fabricius develops a classification system for insects.

1776 English chemist Joseph Priestley synthesises 'laughing gas' – nitrous oxide, later used as an anaesthetic by dentists.

1777 French physicist Charles Coulomb invents the torsion balance, a sensitive device for measuring forces.

but Hussey did not have McCormick's business sense.

In the 1830s, after pioneering work by US blacksmith John Lane, engineers began to make combine harvesters that both cut the wheat and bundled it into sheaves. Separate binding machines were invented, notably by John Appleby in 1878. Later combines also threshed the grain, but the machines needed 10 or more horses to pull them.

↑ This reaper and binder was invented and widely marketed by Cyrus McCormick.

The invention of the steam traction engine and, in 1908, the steam caterpillar tractor overcame this disadvantage. Two years later, petrol-driven combine harvesters began to take over. At first, a separate tractor pulled the harvester; later designers incorporated the motive power as part of the harvesting machine, and ranks of self-propelled combines became a common sight on the prairies.

1778 German-born physician Friedrich Mesmer practises a form of hypnotism known as mesmerism (he is later denounced as a fraud).

1779 Dutch-born British scientist Ian Ingenhousz describes the process of photosynthesis in plants.

1778   1779   1780

1778 English inventor Joseph Bramah patents a flushing toilet.

1779 English weaver Samuel Crompton builds the spinning mule, which twists fibres into yarns and winds them onto bobbins.

1779 Swiss scientist Horace de Saussure coins the term 'geology' for the study of the origin and structure of Earth.

Canals

The main way of moving heavy goods in the late 18th century was by canal. Raw materials and finished goods were transported on barges towed by horses.

⬆ The Bridgewater Canal in northern England was the first modern canal.

TIMELINE
1780–1785

KEY:

Astronomy and Maths

Biology and Medicine

Chemistry and Physics

Engineering and Invention

1780 Italian naturalist Lazzaro Spallanzani carries out artificial insemination on dogs.

1781 French astronomer Charles Messier publishes his Messier catalogue of nebulas and galaxies.

1781 French mineralogist René Haüy suggests that crystals contain 'unit cells', leading to his theory of crystal structure.

1780   1781   1782

1780 American physician Benjamin Rush describes dengue fever.

1782 Scottish engineer James Watt invents a double-acting steam engine in which steam is admitted to each side of the piston alternately.

Chinese engineers built the first canals for transport more than 2,000 years ago. Extensive canal systems were used for drainage and irrigation in northern India, and by the Middle Ages canals were being used in the Netherlands. Canals for industrial transport were first used in England in 1757, after the engineer Henry Berry (1720–1812) completed the Sankey Brook Navigation near St Helens in northern England. The canal at St Helens included a pair of side-by-side locks known as staircase locks.

The First Canals

The first canal of economic importance was the Bridgewater Canal near Manchester, England. It was designed by engineer James Brindley (1716–1772) and completed in 1761. At its narrowest, it was 8 metres (26 feet) wide, and was a contour (gravity-flow) canal with no locks. A canal that takes a more direct route needs locks for coping with inclines, tunnels for going through hills and aqueducts for crossing valleys.

On Brindley's later canals, the locks were just over 4 metres (13 feet) wide. The barges that sailed on these canals therefore had to be narrower than that, but they could be up to 22 metres (72 feet) long – the maximum length of a lock. As a result, they were called

Timeline

1757 Sankey Brook Navigation

1761 Bridgewater Canal

1779 Coteau-du-Lac Canal

1825 Erie Canal

↑ The Bridgewater Canal crossed the Irwell River on a stone viaduct.

1783 English physicist John Michell predicts the existence of 'dark stars', now called black holes.

1784 American scientist and politician Benjamin Franklin invents bifocal eyeglasses.

1783   1784   1785

1783 French brothers Joseph and Jacques Montgolfier invent the hot-air balloon.

1784 French chemist Antoine Lavoisier shows that matter is indestructible, and develops a theory of the conservation of mass.

1784 English scientist Henry Cavendish proves that water is a compound of oxygen and hydrogen, rather than an element.

↑ This lock was built in 1819 on the Grand Junction Canal, which linked London with the manufacturing towns in the Midlands.

narrowboats. They could carry a load of 30 metric tonnes (33 tons), while a wagon could carry just 2 metric tonnes (2.2 tons) and a packhorse's load could not usually exceed about 135 kilograms (300 pounds).

Other canals soon followed. In 1773, the British government commissioned Scottish engineer James Watt (1736–1819) to survey a route in Scotland that would link a series of lochs (saltwater lakes) in order to join the North Sea and the North Atlantic Ocean. Site engineer Thomas Telford (1757–1834), a fellow Scot, began work in 1803, and the first vessel sailed through the canal in 1822. The first canal to take sea-going ships was completed in England in 1819 to connect the south-western town of Exeter with the sea.

↓ The Erie Canal between the Great Lakes and the Hudson River opened in 1825.

Canals in America

In North America, the first canal with locks was

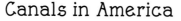

TIMELINE
1785–1790

1785 English inventor Edmund Cartwright makes a steam-powered loom.

1786 German-born English astronomer Caroline Herschel discovers the first of eight comets she will discover in the next 11 years.

KEY:

- Astronomy and Maths
- Biology and Medicine
- Chemistry and Physics
- Engineering and Invention

1785   1786   1787

1785 English physician William Withering introduces the drug digitalis, made from the foxglove plant, to treat heart disorders.

1785 English engineer Robert Ransome invents a cast-iron ploughshare.

1787 German-born English astronomer William Herschel observes Oberon and Titania, two moons of the planet Uranus (which he discovered in 1781).

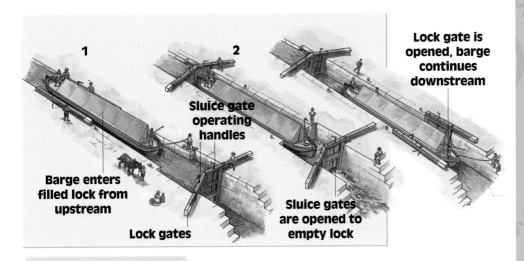

Lock gate is opened, barge continues downstream

1

2

Sluice gate operating handles

Barge enters filled lock from upstream

Lock gates

Sluice gates are opened to empty lock

↑ The pound, or chamber, lock allows canals to rise and fall with the land.

How a pound lock works

A canal lock has a pair of hinged gates at each end, and sluices that can be raised or lowered to let water in and out of the lock. If a boat approaches from upstream, the sluices in the upstream gates are opened until the lock is full of water.
1. The gates open to allow the boat to enter the lock.
2. The gates close and the sluices in the lower gates open until the water level falls to match the level downstream.
3. The gates are opened to allow the boat to exit the lock.

probably the short waterway at Coteau-du-Lac, Quebec, built in 1779 by English engineer William Twiss (1745–1827) in order to bypass a stretch of rough water on the St Lawrence River. In 1825, the Erie Canal was completed to carry grain from the Great Lakes region to New York City via the Hudson River. The 583-kilometre (362-mile) canal was 12 metres (39 feet) wide and 1.2 metres (4 feet) deep and needed 83 locks to cross the high ground west of Troy.

In less than ten years, receipts from tolls more than repaid the $7 million spent on its construction. The enlarged modern canal, which is now part of the New York State canal system, can carry barges of up to 2,000 metric tonnes (2,204 tons).

1788 French mathematician Joseph Lagrange publishes a book analysing the calculus of mechanics.

1789 English clergyman Gilbert White publishes *The Natural History and Antiquities of Selborne*, a wildlife guide that is still read today.

1788

1789

1790

1788 Scottish engineer William Symington builds a steam paddleboat.

1789 German chemist Martin Klaproth discovers uranium and zirconium.

1789 French physician Joseph Guillotin invents the guillotine, which is used from 1792 for executions during the French Revolution.

Railways

Railways had their origins in the 16th century, when miners in Europe used horses to pull wagons along 'roads' of beams of timber laid lengthways on the ground.

↞ A locomotive crosses a boggy region west of Manchester in northern England.

TIMELINE
1790–1795

KEY:

- Astronomy and Maths
- Biology and Medicine
- Chemistry and Physics
- Engineering and Invention

1790 Claude and Ignace Chappe, from France, invent a telegraph that uses two movable arms to signal letters of the alphabet.

1791 French mineralogist Déodat de Dolomieu discovers the mineral dolomite.

1792 Scottish engineer William Murdock uses coal gas for domestic lighting.

1790

1791

1792

1790 French chemist Nicolas Leblanc invents a process for making soda (calcium carbonate) from salt.

In the 16th and 17th centuries, miners in Europe used carts on wooden rails to move coal. When Abraham Darby began making cheap cast iron in the early 1700s, stronger cast-iron rails became more available.

↑ Trevithick's locomotive of 1803 used iron wheels running on iron rails.

Steam Enters the Scene

The first steam locomotive was built in 1803 by English engineer Richard Trevithick. The locomotive and rolling stock had unflanged wheels, but there was a lip on the outer edge of the track. Four years later, he built a circular track in London and charged people a shilling (5p) to ride on his train – called *Catch Me Who Can*.

The first railway to regularly carry passengers as well as freight opened in 1825. With locomotives built by English engineer George Stephenson, the Stockton & Darlington Railway ran for 42 kilometres (26 miles). The first inter-city line, the Liverpool & Manchester Railway, opened in 1830, and the first train was hauled by Stephenson's *Rocket*. Built mainly to carry cotton from the port of Liverpool to the mills

↑ This drawing shows the opening of the Stockton & Darlington Railway in 1825.

Stephenson's Rocket

The most famous early locomotive was the *Rocket*, built by Robert and George Stephenson. *Rocket* improved on earlier models and set the pattern for later steam trains. Some people worried that passengers would not be able to breathe in the rushing air.

in Manchester in the north-west of England, the line had to cross an extensive bog. Stephenson (who was also the railway's chief construction engineer) overcame the problem by building it on compacted hurdles 'floating' on the waterlogged ground.

Railways also sprang up in other countries. In the United States, the year 1830 saw the inauguration of the Baltimore & Ohio Railroad, which initially ran for 21 kilometres (13 miles) from Baltimore to Ellicott's Mills. The longest railway in the world at the time, the South Carolina Railroad, started operations in 1831. It ran for 248 kilometres (154 miles) from Charleston to Hamburg. France and Germany got their first railways in 1832 and 1835, respectively. By 1840, there were railways in Austria, Ireland and the Netherlands. As the new railways appeared, barges disappeared and canals fell into disrepair.

← The *Rocket* won trials to become the locomotive on the first inter-city line.

Changing the Tracks

As well as locomotives and rolling stock, railways need other equipment. The 'way' of the original railways employed iron

TIMELINE
1795–1800

1795 Scottish geologist James Hutton publishes his ideas on the history of Earth, which form the basis of modern geology.

1796 French astronomer Pierre-Simon de Laplace suggests that the sun and planets condensed out of a swirling mass of gas.

1797 The mineral chromium is discovered, followed by strontium in 1798.

KEY:

Astronomy and Maths

Biology and Medicine

Chemistry and Physics

Engineering and Invention

1795

1796

1797

1795 English inventor Joseph Bramah invents a hydraulic press.

1796 German physician Franz Gall introduces phrenology, which relates mental ability to the shape of the head – the theory is now discounted.

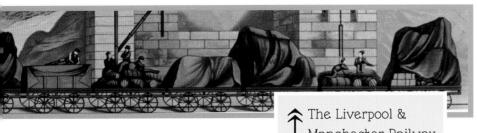

The Liverpool & Manchester Railway carried freight as well as passengers.

As chief engineer of the Liverpool & Manchester Railway, George Stephenson was responsible for designing and building structures such as this tunnel.

rails. They were made of cast iron, at first with a right-angled section to keep the wheels on the track. Soon, these flanged rails were replaced. The flanges were put on the wheels of the vehicles, which ran on short 'fish-bellied' rails that were straight on top but curved beneath to make them thicker (and stronger) in the centre. But cast-iron rails were brittle and often broke. From 1858, they were replaced by steel rails.

Railway points were invented as early as 1789 for tramway systems. Once trains started running into each other, signals were invented in the form of discs or arms that rotated or pivoted. In 1849, the New York and Erie Company introduced block signalling, which does not allow a train to enter a section of track until the previous train has left it. Eventually, block signals were linked electrically. Within a few decades, railways would cover vast distances.

1798 English economist Thomas Malthus discovers a correlation between the size of a population and the available food supply: the former always increases more quickly than the latter.

1799 English scientists Thomas Beddoes and Humphry Davy conduct experiments using laughing gas (nitrous oxide).

1798   1799   1800

1798 Danish mathematician Caspar Wessel represents complex numbers as vectors (quantities with magnitude and direction).

1799 American-born British scientist Benjamin Thompson helps found the Royal Institution in London.

1800 English astronomer William Herschel discovers infrared radiation (from the sun).

Glossary

bellows A flexible air chamber that is pumped to create a stream of air to produce a draught for a fire or furnace.

cast iron A type of iron containing a lot of carbon, which is too hard to be shaped and so is moulded, or cast, in the shape required.

chronometer An extremely accurate mechanical clock, used for finding ships' longitude at sea.

comet A small, icy body in orbit around the sun.

element Any substance that cannot be split chemically into simpler substances.

flange A projecting rim that sticks out from a roller or rail to act as a guide.

furnace An enclosed chamber in which fire is used to produce very high temperatures for smelting metals.

governor A mechanical device that automatically regulates the speed of a machine.

horsepower A measurement of power, originally developed by James Watt to measure the power of steam engines against that of draughthorses.

latitude The distance of a point on the globe north or south of the equator, measured as an angle.

lightning conductor A metal rod placed on top of a tall structure to protect it by attracting lightning strikes and carrying the charge harmlessly to the ground.

lock A stretch of a canal enclosed by gates to control the water level and raise or lower boats passing through it.

longitude The distance of a point on the globe east or west of the prime meridian, measured as an angle.

meridian An imaginary line of longitude that circles Earth from the North to the South Pole; the prime meridian, or $0°$, passes through Greenwich, England.

reaping The process of cutting a crop in order to harvest it.

rolling stock The carriages and wagons pulled by a locomotive.

treadle A foot-operated rocker that drives mechanical motion.

vacuum A completely empty space in which there is no air.

Further Reading

Books

Bingham, Jane. *The Story of Trains.* Usborne Publishing Ltd, 2005.

Birch, Beverley. *Adventures with Electricity: Benjamin Franklin's Story.* Mathew Price Ltd, 2013.

Borden, Louise. *Sea Clocks: The Story of Longitude.* National Maritime Museum, 2008.

Deary, Terry. *Vile Victorians* (Horrible History). Scholastic Non-Fiction, 2011.

Gifford, Clive. *The Industrial Revolution* (The Who's Who of...). Wayland, 2013.

Hall, Margaret C. *Eli Whitney* (Lives and Times). Heinemann Library, 2004.

Hepplewhite, Peter. *The Industrial Revolution* (All About). Wayland, 2002.

Hepplewhite, Peter. *Awfully Ancient: Thomas Crapper, Corsets and Cruel Britannia.* Wayland, 2014.

Hewitt, Sallly. *Brunel the Great Engineer* (Ways Into History). Franklin Watts, 2012.

Royston, Angela. *Inventors Who Changed the World.* A&C Black Publishers, 2011.

Smith, Nigel. *The Industrial Revolution* (Events and Outcomes). Evans Brothers Ltd, 2009.

Websites

www.bbc.co.uk/history/british/ victorians/launch_ani_rocket.shtml
BBC animation of the Rocket.

http://www.famousscientists.org/ benjamin-franklin/
An account of Benjamin Franklin's career as a scientist.

inventors.about.com/library/ inventors/blsteamengine.htm
About.com site about the invention of the steam engine, with links to biographies.

www.saburchill.com/history/ chapters/IR/001.html
The Open Door website page on the Industrial Revolution, with many links.

Note to parents and teachers concerning websites: In the book every effort has been made by the Publishers to ensure that websites are suitable for children, that they are of the highest educational value, and that they contain no inappropriate or offensive material. However, because of the nature of the Internet, it is impossible to guarantee that the contents of these sites will not be altered. We advise that Internet access is supervised by a responsible adult.

Index